Jessica Joins the Band

This edition was published by The Dreamwork Collective

The Dreamwork Collective LLC, Dubai, United Arab Emirates

thedreamworkcollective.com

Printed and bound in the United Arab Emirates by Al Ghurair Printing & Publishing

Text © Jessica Smith, 2022

Illustrations © Hasīna Shafad, 2022

Design © Alexandra Andrieș, 2022

ISBN 978-9948-8821-3-8

MC-02-01-7392898

Age Classification E

The content of this book is appropriate according to the age classification system issued by the Ministry of Culture and Youth.

All rights reserved. No part of this publication may be reproduced, stored, or transmitted in any form or by any means, electronic, mechanical, photo-copying, recording, or otherwise, without prior permission of the publishers. The right of Jessica Smith to be identified as the author of this work has been asserted and protected under the UAE Copyright and Authorship Protection Law No. 7.

Dedicated to my beautiful children,
who inspire me every day to be a better version of myself.

And to everyone who has been made to feel as though
their differences were anything but a superpower . . .

Your differences are what illuminates this world.

Jessica Joins the Band

written by Jessica Smith
illustrated by Hasīna Shafad

THE
DREAMWORK
COLLECTIVE

Jessica woke up extra early because she was so excited.
Today she is trying out for the school band.

Jessica loves music.

Jessica had only ever played the recorder,
but she dreamed of playing the drums in the school band.

"Are you excited about trying out for the school band?" asked Mum.

"Yes! I'm so excited, I love music," said Jessica.

"Will you be playing the recorder today?" asked Mum.

"No", said Jessica cheerfully, "I'm going to play the drums!"

"The drums!" shrieked Jessica's dad.

Jessica's brothers started banging on pots and pans.

"That's not music!" exclaimed Jessica, "that's just loud noise!"

"Let me show you!"
Jessica started tapping on the pots with a wooden spoon, and it sounded amazing.

Once Jessica had finished eating her breakfast, she was ready to go to school.

When Jessica arrived at school, she went straight to the music room.

Her friends were talking about what instruments they wanted to play in the school band.

"I'm going to play the guitar," said Zahra.

"I want to play the piano," said Fabio, "I love music!"

"Me too," said Jessica excitedly, "I'm going to play the drums!"

"The drums? You can't play the drums," said Grace. "You need two hands to play the drums!" declared James.

"You can do lots of things, but maybe the drums will be too hard for you?" whispered Fabio.

"Why don't we ask the music teacher what instruments you can play with one hand?"

"Jessica why don't you try playing the trumpet!" said Jessica's music teacher. "It's a brass instrument and the three buttons on top are called valves."

Jessica had never seen a trumpet before. She blew really hard while holding down one of the valves. It sounded a bit funny.

Jessica felt embarrassed.

"What about the piano?" said Fabio, "we can play it together."

Jessica smiled while she sat next to Fabio playing the piano.

But to be in the band, everyone needed to play their own instrument.

Jessica really wanted to play the drums, it's what she had always dreamed to do.

Jessica's music teacher could see that she was feeling upset.

"You CAN play the drums," he said, "you just have to find your own way of doing it."

Jessica picked up one of the drumsticks and sat down ready to play.

"You might not be able to use both drumsticks, but you can still use one, and you can also use your foot to play the kickdrum," said Jessica's music teacher.

Jessica started playing, using one drumstick while her foot tapped away at the kickdrum.

Jessica's teacher explained how to time her hand and feet to create a beat.

It sounded awesome.

All the kids were amazed at how well Jessica could play the drums!

"Wow!" shouted James, "you are playing the drums with only one hand!"

Jessica's teacher asked everyone to get their instruments ready, and the kids started playing together.

The band had been formed!

Jessica was full of joy.

She believed in herself even when others said she couldn't do it.

She remembered what her teacher had said, she just needed to find her own way of doing it.

When Jessica got home she was so excited to tell her parents about playing in the school band.

"How was your day?" asked Mum.
"My day was great, I love music so much! I played the drums in the school band!" said Jessica.

"I'm so proud of you," said Mum.

"Did you learn anything today?" asked Dad.

"I sure did," said Jessica. "I learnt that I can do anything, I just need to find my own way of doing it."

".... Does this mean I need to buy a drum kit?" asked Dad, putting his hands over his ears.

the end

Continue the conversation . . .

What's something you dream of doing?

Also in the *Just Jessica* series:

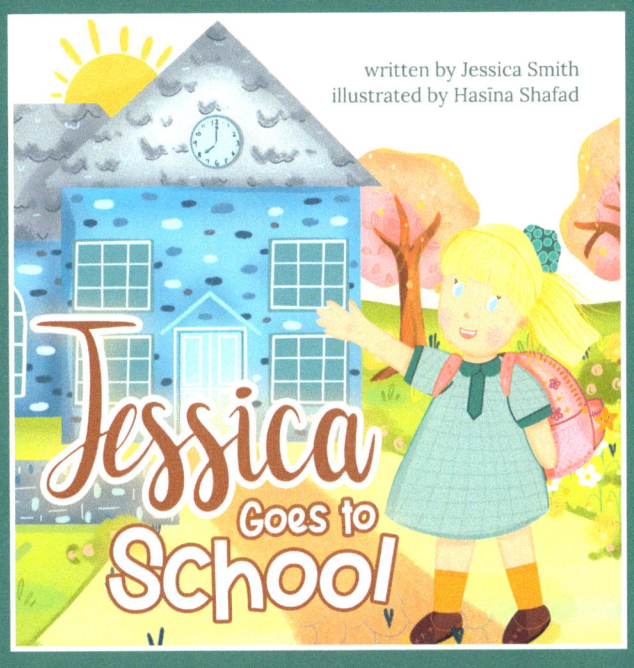
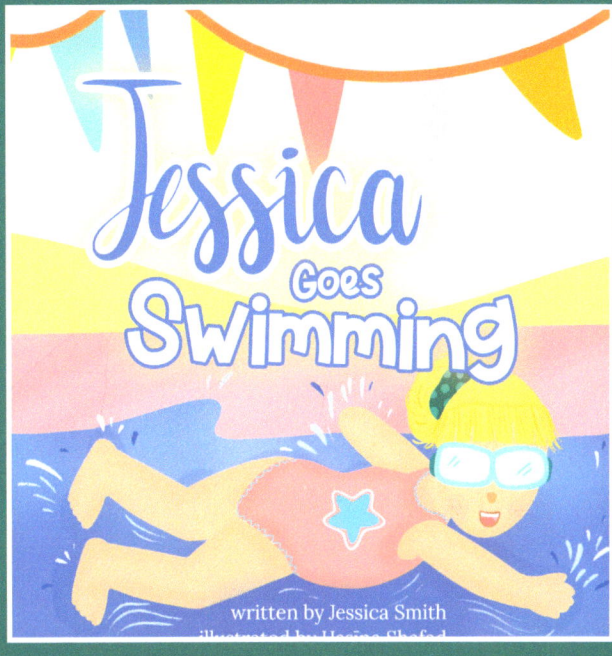

Author Bio – Jessica Smith

Jessica was born and raised in Australia, but now calls Dubai home. Born missing her left arm, Jessica focused her energy on sport and exercise as a way of proving to the world that she could overcome perceived limitations. She went on to become a Paralympic swimmer and represented Australia for 7 years. Jessica is now an internationally recognised inclusion and diversity expert and the Chief Operating Officer at TOUCH Dubai. Through the Just Jessica series, the mother of 3 wants to encourage important conversations about the beauty of difference.

 @jessicasmith27

Illustrator Bio - Hasīna Shafad

Hasīna is an illustrator and artist based in Dubai. From cute stickers to wedding stationery and children's books, she loves to create colourful and cozy art that reflects the world around her. When she is not working, she enjoys reading, traveling, cooking and spending time with her beautiful family.

 **@turquoiseluna**

Sponsor – Jean Winter

Jean Winter is the CEO of Jean Winter Consultancy and TOUCH Dubai. TOUCH Dubai is paving the way for a more inclusive world through its disability and inclusion consultancy and talent management agency. Based in the United Arab Emirates, it brings together people with remarkable stories that need to be shared with the world and represents people from various industries with the goal of creating a more inclusive paradigm for society and businesses.

 @touchdubai

Publisher – The Dreamwork Collective

The Dreamwork Collective is a print and digital publisher sharing diverse voices and powerful stories with the world. Dedicated to the advancement of humanity, we strive to create books that have a positive impact on people and on the planet. Our hope is that our books document this moment in time for future generations to enjoy and learn from, and that we play our part in ushering humanity into a new era of heightened creativity, connection, and compassion.

www.ingramcontent.com/pod-product-compliance
Lightning Source LLC
LaVergne TN
LVHW070435070526
838199LV00015B/514